You Deserve to be Loved by You!

31 Daily Affirmations for Building Confidence and Boosting Self-Esteem

LESLIE TUCKER

You Deserve to be Loved by You!

Cover creation courtesy of Ravi Verma from rdezines.com

Editing and formatting courtesy of Lorraine Reguly from https://WordingWell.com

Contents

Preface

Who was the stranger in the mirror? She was not lost because she never found herself. She acted in ways unlike herself. She wanted to feel the love she craved so badly. She went out of her way to people-please. But she was the one who was never at ease.

Who was "she"? She was me.

I questioned everything about myself.

Am I good enough? Am I too nice? Am I nice enough? Should I smile more often? Am I too strong? Am I too independent? Am I likable? Am I lovable? Do I deserve greatness?

I feel different. I think differently. I act differently. I have different experiences. I don't always fit in. I question myself, constantly.

Why me? Am I right or am I wrong? Does anyone understand me?

Does any of this sound familiar?

It's draining to feel this way every day… always wondering if we are good enough.

But we can feel good about ourselves, regardless of what others think, if we are determined to be the confident and self-loving women we were born to be!

Self-love is an intentional journey which takes time, practice, and patience, but we are worth the time and effort.

No one is perfect, and that's okay. Repeat these affirmations every day, in any order. It may take days or even months before you start to believe them, as change does not happen overnight, but it will happen. Trust me.

My dear, you are beautiful, smart, talented, cherished, important special, worthy, and loved. Don't allow anyone to tell you otherwise.

The self-love and confidence journey starts now.

Affirmation #1: I Am Enough

I was enough yesterday, I am enough today, and I will continue to be enough tomorrow.

I was created with everything I need for greatness. Sure, there's always room for improvement, but I know the difference between self-growth and not loving myself. I am working on becoming the best version of myself while loving myself throughout the process.

I am enough the way I am. My relationships, my productivity and my accomplishments don't determine my worth. I am enough because I am me, and there is only one of me.

Leslie Tucker

Affirmation #2: I Think and Speak Highly of Myself

I only speak positive and uplifting words about myself, and to myself. I don't put myself down because of my mistakes, nor do I call myself names like fat, skinny, stupid, or crazy. I call myself what I am: a queen, blessed, smart, beautiful, and amazing.

I think and speak highly of myself. Speaking highly of myself does not mean I am conceited or arrogant; it means I love myself and believe in myself. If I do not think and speak highly of myself, I cannot expect others to do the same.

What I project is what I will attract, and I attract greatness.

Leslie Tucker

Affirmation #3: I Am Free to Be Myself

I do not pretend to be someone I am not. I took off the mask and I like what I see. I see someone who is comfortable in her skin.

I am okay with the fact that I am different. I dance to my own beat. I no longer hold back parts of my personality, uniqueness, and quirks just to try to fit into someone else's mold.

I let go of who I was trying to be, and became who I really am. I am playful and serious; sweet and sassy; adventurous and a homebody; stable and moody.

I embrace it all. I am free to be me.

Affirmation #4: I Will Not Blame Myself for Other's Actions

I will not blame myself for what happened to me. Although family, romantic partners, bosses, and others have let me down, I will not blame myself for their actions.

I can't control what others think, speak and how they react. I can only control myself and the way I react to them.

I do not internalize others' actions anymore. I will no longer make other people's issues my own. I will use that same energy to love myself and continue to become the best version of myself. If someone leaves or disrespects me, I will let them go and know it is their loss.

People's actions are a reflection of their feelings, perspective, and character—not me.

Affirmation #5: I Am Whole

I am not looking for someone to "complete me." I am already a whole person.

I truly enjoy friendships, companionship, and relationships, but I will not seek them merely to complete myself. I understand if I am looking for someone to complete me because I feel lonely, I am putting myself in a position to settle.

I know the best friendships, companions, and relationships are formed when two whole people come together. I was created to be pleased with myself. I am already whole.

I love myself and will treat myself like the whole person that I am. I am not broken. I love myself regardless of my past.

Leslie Tucker

Affirmation #6: I Am Gifted and Talented

I was born with gifts and talents—even if I have not yet discovered them yet.

I do not have to do what is popular in order to be talented.

I understand my gifts and talents may be writing, dancing, singing, listening, teaching, speaking, crafting, building, sports, painting, drawing, humor, planning, performing, baking, fitness, storytelling, encouraging, acting, graphic design, and organizing, etc.

When I discover my gifts and talents, I will be proud of them. I will not try to be like someone else.

I understand that I was born with these gifts for a reason, which is to help people and enrich my own life.

I will not let my gifts and talents go to waste. I believe in my abilities. The world is waiting for what I have to offer it.

Leslie Tucker

Affirmation #7: I Will Not Live a Life of Regret

I will work towards my heart's desires. I will write a book, start a business, move across the country, go back to school, give love another try, speak my mind, and cut my hair.

I will say "NO" when I want to.

I will not live my life based on what others want me to do. I will go to bed each night knowing that I did what I wanted to do. I will feel a sense of accomplishment at the end of each day.

I know that no matter how old I am or how much time has passed, I can still pursue my dreams. I will not live a life of regret.

Affirmation #8: I Will Allow Myself to Be Happy

I choose to wake up looking for the good in each day. I know that bad things sometimes happen that I cannot control, but I will not let it ruin my day.

I deserve happiness and I allow myself to feel happy. I will not allow my past to block today's goodness.

I understand that happiness is a choice and I choose happiness because it feels better.

I will allow myself to fall in love with the right person, pursue my dreams, and live in the moment so I may enjoy my life.

I do not let fear, guilt, and/or shame steal my happiness anymore.

Affirmation #9: I Live Each Day to the Fullest

I am happy to be alive and I will live each day to the fullest.

Tomorrow is not promised, so I will have fun, take chances, and embrace each day. I look for the small moments daily that later end up being big moments.

I take opportunities that come my way, instead of always playing it safe.

I take risks. I do not limit myself. I step outside of my comfort zone and I am proud of myself for it.

I go to bed each night knowing that I made the most of my day.

Affirmation #10: I Will Never Give Up on Myself

I believe in my greatness.

I may try and fail sometimes, and I do not always get my way, but I will never ever give up on myself, my goals, or my dreams. My mistakes are learning experiences that teach me and build my character. If I mess up, I will try again. I will tell myself "Day One," instead of "one day."

I am too smart, determined, and deserving to give up on myself. I do not allow failure to get the best of me. Starting today, I will get back up when I fall and remember I am here to win.

I am stronger than any deflating moment life throws at me. I will never give up on myself.

Leslie Tucker

Affirmation #11: I Am Grateful

I have so much to be grateful for. Of course, things could always be better and I will continue to work for what I want. How could I ask for more, if I am not grateful for what I already have?

I remain grateful for everything I have in the present moment. I know there are people who wish they could have what I have. I understand that if what I have was taken away from me, I would be devastated. So, I wake up every morning grateful for my life and everything in it.

I wake up every morning choosing gratitude. On the days I may forget everything I am grateful for, I remind myself that I am grateful to be alive and I have been given another chance to show my gratitude.

Leslie Tucker

Affirmation#12: I Have Come So Far

I have come so far from where I started. I may not be exactly where I want to be, yet, but I am proud of where I am and my accomplishments.

I have accomplished things that once seemed impossible. I overcame challenges others did not even know I had. I celebrate how far I have come, rather than being upset over not being where I want to be.

I am still growing. I have come so far and I will keep going.

Affirmation #13: I Am Easy to Love

I am a beautiful, loving person and I am easy to love.

I will not let the love I did not receive from another person make me feel unlovable. I will not internalize when someone does not reciprocate the love I give.

My mistakes, my past, and my imperfections do not make me unlovable. I deserve love and I am worthy of it, regardless of where I come from or what I have been through.

Most of all, I am easy to love because I love myself and that is the best kind of love there is.

Leslie Tucker

Affirmation #14: I Am Beautiful, Inside and Out

My beauty comes from within. This makes me beautiful, inside and out.

I am beautiful because I am me.

My beauty shows in the way I think, act, and speak.

My beauty is not determined by what others think of me. My heart is beautiful, my mind is beautiful, and my soul is beautiful. When I look in the mirror I see a masterpiece.

I choose to focus on what I love about myself, instead of what I think is wrong with me. There is always room for growth, but I am still beautiful in the process.

I choose to see the beauty in myself because I am beautiful, inside and out.

Affirmation #15: I Enjoy My Own Company

I enjoy my own company. I am fun, creative, and interesting. My imagination goes as far as I allow it.

I enjoy my own company because I am happy with myself. I love myself; therefore, I can sit alone with myself. I love to be around good people, but I am just as happy by myself.

When I am alone, I use that time to grow, think, and be good to myself. I make plans for my future while enjoying the present. I use that time to be grateful for everything I am and everything I am becoming.

I know that one of the best things I can do for myself is to enjoy ME. I am with myself 24/7, 365 days a year, so I have learned to enjoy my own company.

Leslie Tucker

Affirmation #16: I Trust My Gut

I trust my judgment and the intuition that I was born with. My gut feelings are there to protect and guide me through life.

I do not ignore my gut just because I want to date someone or take a risk that I know is not good for me. I do not ignore red flags anymore. Instead, I trust that what is meant for me will come naturally and I will not have to chase it down.

I will wait for what's best for me and my future. I listen to my heart and mind, but I trust my gut.

Affirmation #17: I Deserve True Love

I deserve the purest love there is.

I deserve respect, honesty, compassion, loyalty, and someone who is here for me. I do not deserve lies, disrespect, foolery, or someone who is just looking for a good time with me.

I have a lot to offer my future love, and he has a lot to offer me. I will not entertain "good enough" when there is someone amazing out there who is looking and praying to find me.

I attract healthy and meaningful relationships into my life now, and I will choose my relationships wisely, because I know what I deserve.

Affirmation #18: I Can and I Will

I can and I will do anything and everything I put my mind to.

Whatever my heart desires is—or will be—mine.

I am capable of achieving whatever I want.

I can do what seems impossible because I am strong, determined, and worthy of every amazing thing that life has to offer.

I do not sit around waiting for opportunities to find me and then get upset when it does not happen. I create the life I want to live and create my own opportunities. Goodness chases me down and I remain open to receive it.

I can and I will be the extraordinarily amazing person I was created to be.

Affirmation #19: I Am Confident

I think very highly of myself and I am sure of myself.

I no longer allow self-doubt stick around. I trust myself. I am not perfect, but I believe in myself and my decisions. If I make a mistake, I learn from it and bounce back.

I enter every situation feeling good about myself and I am not inferior to others.

If have a bad day, I remember who I am and where I am going because I am confident in myself and my abilities.

Leslie Tucker

Affirmation #20: My Past Does Not Define Me

My past had to happen or I would not be the woman I love today.

My past is a part of my story, but it is not who I am. I am not what happened to me. I am not who left me. I am not the situation I accidentally dragged myself into.

My past was used as a lesson to make me wiser and more knowledgeable so I can help others. My past has helped me grow as a person and I am not ashamed of it anymore.

My past is behind me. My past does not define me. I've grown and I am moving on.

Affirmation #21: I Do Not Look Back

I look and move ahead, not backwards.

The present moment is here now and my future is ahead of me. I look forward to all the good that is coming to me and that is here right now.

I say goodbye to everything that did not work out for me, and I do not continue to mourn what was lost. I am grateful for everything that did not work out for me. If a person or missed opportunity is gone, it was not mine to begin with.

There are many jobs, potential romantic partners and countless opportunities waiting for me.

I leave the past where it is and I do not look back.

Affirmation #22: I Respect Myself

I respect myself. Therefore, I only allow people around me who respect me as well.

I take care of my mind, body, and soul. I allow myself time to rest. I exercise and I spend time feeding my soul.

I do not let others run over me out of fear they may leave me, nor do I tolerate disrespect just so I may keep someone's company. Instead, I speak my truth and avoid people and things that do not uplift me.

I will not engage in harmful and reckless behavior to self-soothe, after a bad day. I will continue to practice self-care and self-love, out of self-respect.

Leslie Tucker

Affirmation #23: I Remain True to Myself

If I want it, I will go after it. If I do not want it, I will say "NO."

I am pursuing my dreams and will continue to do so.

I am authentic. I do not act out of my character, to try to fit in. I will not hide parts of my personality to try to make someone else happy.

I have integrity in all that I do.

I set boundaries and I stick with them. I have standards and I uphold them.

I am not a people-pleaser anymore. I no longer allow others to influence me. I know, at the end of the day, I have to live with every decision I make, so I remain true to myself.

Affirmation #24: I Trust and Enjoy My Life's Journey

I am exactly where I am supposed to be in life. If I wasn't, I would be somewhere else.

My life has been full of ups, downs, and surprises. Yes, I have been disappointed and let down, but I know I am on the right track because God has a plan for my life.

I enter each phase of life ready to learn and grow. Sometimes things happen that I do not like. However, I know that whatever I am presented with, I will get through.

Because of my journey, I am stronger, wiser, and well-equipped to handle all the good (and bad) that comes my way.

Affirmation #25: I Am One of a Kind

I am one of a kind.

There is only one me and that is what makes me special. My height, my weight, my hair color and texture, my skin, my eyes, and my curves are all mine.

I love my personality, my quirks, and everything about me that makes me stand out.

I am not meant to be like anyone other than myself.

I am happy with myself, and I do not wish I was someone else. I am one of a kind.

Affirmation #26: My Life is Meaningful

I inspire myself and others. I am here to do great things.

My life's meaning does not come from my relationship status, my job, or from everything I wish I was. My life has meaning because of who I am today.

My life has meaning. Because I still have air in my lungs, this means I am not done.

I am happy to be alive and I bring light and positivity to everything I touch.

Affirmation #27: I Am Strong

I am proud to be a strong woman.

I do not buckle under pressure and I persevere in everything I do. Yes, I feel scared sometimes. Yes, at times, I need to ask for help. Neither means I am weak. Asking for help is actually a sign of strength.

My strength comes from believing in myself. My body is strong, my mind is strong, and my soul is strong.

Being strong is asking for help when needed and not allowing my ego to win. Being strong is expressing my emotions and crying if I need to, but still handling business. It is not making excuses and complaining all the time about why my life is the way it is.

Being strong is also getting up every day when I do not feel like it, and doing my best all over again.

Some may feel uncomfortable with my strength and that is okay. I am proud to be strong because I was made that way.

Affirmation #28: I Am Successful Right Now

I am successful at this very moment.

There are things I still want to accomplish, and I am still working towards my goals, but that does not make me any less successful right now.

I am proud of myself for all of the goals I have already accomplished. I am proud at how far I have come.

I celebrate the small victories in my life because they will eventually lead to big victories.

My success is not measured by where I am now, but how dedicated I am to achieving my goals. It is also not measured by how much money I make, how popular I am, or what kind of car I drive.

When I look at the progress I have made, I am proud to say that I am successful right now.

Affirmation #29: I Do Not Compare Myself to Others

I do not compare myself to others because I am unique and special in my own way.

I came into this world to be myself at all times, and I am creating the life I want to live.

I do not want to be like anyone else or live someone else's life, because that would not be authentic of me. Comparing myself to others is harmful and a waste of time because God did not make a mistake when he created me.

I love my life, and I am becoming the best version of myself while being me.

Affirmation #30: I Will Not Settle for "Good Enough" When I Know I Deserve More

In a world of "here and now," I will not settle for "good enough," when I know I deserve more.

I will not settle in relationships, friendships, work, or any other aspect of life.

I will not settle for any romantic partner just because I'm alone, lonely, or because I love him. I will continue to better myself while I am in the process of finding true love and companionship. I understand that settling for love will only leave me with heartache, pain, and regret. From this point on, I am selective with whom I decide to share my heart.

I will not settle for friendships filled with toxicity and disrespect. I choose my circle of friends wisely and I will only surround myself with people who are like-minded. My friendship circle is filled with honestly, loyalty, and positivity. We uplift each other and want to see the other grow.

I will not settle for a job I am not happy with. I work eight hours a day and I will be satisfied throughout my workday. I will not settle at work when it comes to pay, respect, or my dignity. I will work somewhere that feels right for me, or I will work for myself. I understand that I may not be fulfilled now, but I have the power to change that. I will work in a way that makes every day feel like a Friday, and I'm not sad on Monday mornings.

I will not settle for less than I deserve.

Affirmation #31: I Am Not Perfect and That's Okay

I am not perfect and that's okay.

I make mistakes. I sometimes say weird things. Occasionally, my thoughts run all over the place. All of these things are okay. I understand that my value has nothing to do with being perfect.

I am a good person. Each day, I do my very best and that is enough.

I was created to be me, which makes me amazing.

I do not want to be perfect because it is unrealistic and involves too much pressure. My imperfections give me room to grow as a person and lessons to learn.

I love myself. I am not perfect and that's okay.

A Note from the Author

Thank you for reading!

For more inspiration, follow me on social media and subscribe to my blog:

Up and Forward on Purpose:
https://upandforwardonpurpose.com

Pinterest:
https://www.pinterest.com/upandforwardon
purpose/

Instagram:
https://www.instagram.com/ms_leslie_tucke
r/

Twitter:
https://twitter.com/UpAndForwardLA

I appreciate each and every share with others!

About the Author

Leslie Tucker is a writer who was born and raised in Los Angeles, California. She discovered her love for writing at four years old and was determined to become an author. She is a Christian who enjoys reading, baking, swimming, volunteering, and dark chocolate. Leslie is the mother of three (two boys and a girl). A German Shepherd named Moe is also part of her family.

Leslie is also the creator of the **Up and Forward on Purpose** blog. In May 2019, Leslie was nominated for the Sunshine Blogger Award for spreading positivity and light in her writings.

Leslie lost her father when she was 13 years old. After ending a 14-year marriage and spending most of her adult life trying to be "happy," she realized happiness begins with self-love. She made it her mission to learn what it means to truly love herself and feel confident. She shares her knowledge with the world in many ways, including via her website and her book, *You Deserve to Be Loved by You!*

Leslie believes in the power of positive thinking. She believes our words have power and that what we tell ourselves, we believe.

She went from ruminating over past mistakes and failures to showing herself compassion and uplifting herself with affirmations.

You can learn more about Leslie at https://upandforwardonpurpose.com and can connect with her on Pinterest at https://www.pinterest.com/upandforwardon purpose/, on Instagram at https://www.instagram.com/ms_leslie_tucke r/, and on Twitter at https://twitter.com/UpAndForwardLA.